CRASHED

GREAT DEPRESSION

Virginia Loh-Hagan

45TH PARALLEL PRESS

Published in the United States of America by Cherry Lake Publishing
Ann Arbor, Michigan
www.cherrylakepublishing.com

Reading Adviser: Marla Conn, MS, Ed., Literacy specialist, Read-Ability Inc.
Cover Designer: Felicia Macheske

Photo Credits: © Lange, Dorothea, photographer., 1938. Jan. Photograph., Library of Congress,
https://www.loc.gov/item/2017770696/, cover, 1; © Everett Historical/Shutterstock.com, 5, 6, 11, 12,
17, 18, 23, 25, 29; © Library of Congress, LC-F8- 4556, 21

Graphic Elements Throughout: © Chipmunk131/Shutterstock.com; © Nowik Sylwia/Shutterstock.com;
© Andrey_Popov/Shutterstock.com; © NadzeyaShanchuk/Shutterstock.com; © KathyGold/Shutterstock.com;
© Black creator/Shutterstock.com; © Edvard Molnar/Shutterstock.com; © Elenadesign/Shutterstock.com;
© estherpoon/Shutterstock.com

Copyright © 2020 by Cherry Lake Publishing
All rights reserved. No part of this book may be reproduced or utilized in any
form or by any means without written permission from the publisher.

45th Parallel Press is an imprint of Cherry Lake Publishing.

Library of Congress Cataloging-in-Publication Data

Names: Loh-Hagan, Virginia, author.
Title: Crashed : Great Depression / Virginia Loh-Hagan.
Description: Ann Arbor, Michigan : Cherry Lake Publishing, [2020]. | Series: Behind the curtain | Includes index.
Identifiers: LCCN 2019032893 | ISBN 9781534159440 (hardcover) | ISBN 9781534161740 (paperback) |
    ISBN 9781534160590 (pdf) | ISBN 9781534162891 (ebook)
Subjects: LCSH: United States–History–1933-1945–Juvenile literature. | United States–History–1919-1933–Juvenile
    literature. | Depressions–1929–United States–Juvenile literature.
Classification: LCC E806 .L644 2020 | DDC 973.917–dc23
LC record available at https://lccn.loc.gov/2019032893

Cherry Lake Publishing would like to acknowledge the work of the Partnership for 21st Century Learning,
a Network of Battelle for Kids. Please visit *http://www.battelleforkids.org/networks/p21* for more information.

Printed in the United States of America
Corporate Graphics

A Note on Dramatic Retellings

Participating in Readers Theater, or dramatic retellings, can greatly improve reading skills, especially fluency. The books in the **BEHIND THE CURTAIN** series give readers opportunities to learn about important historical events in a fun and engaging way. These books serve as a bridge to more complex texts. All the characters are real figures from history; however, their stories have been fictionalized. To learn more about the people and the events, check out the Viewpoints and Perspectives series and the Perspectives Library series, as the **BEHIND THE CURTAIN** books are aligned to these stories.

TABLE of CONTENTS

HISTORICAL BACKGROUND

The Great Depression lasted from 1929 to 1939. The stock market crashed on October 24, 1929. This was the start of the Great Depression. It was known as Black Thursday. October 29, 1929, was called Black Tuesday. Panic set in. Stocks fell. Prices dropped. People stopped shopping. Unsold goods piled up. Factories slowed down. Workers were fired.

During the Great Depression, the banking system was weak. Farm prices were low. Then dust storms hit farmlands. This was called the Dust Bowl. Dust and drought caused crops to die. Farmers couldn't grow food.

FLASH FACT!

Crowds gathered in shock outside the New York Stock Exchange during the 1929 crash.

Vocabulary

depression (dih-PRESH-uhn) a long and severe slump or downturn in the economy

stock market (STAHK MAHR-kit) a system where traders buy and sell shares of companies

drought (DROUT) period of low rainfall

FLASH FACT!

The Great Depression affected other countries.

Vocabulary

starved (STAHRVD) had extreme hunger

breadlines (BRED-linez) lines of people waiting to get free bread or other food

soup kitchens (SOOP KICH-uhnz) places where people can get free food

economy (ih-KAH-nuh-mee) the wealth and resources of a country

Banks went out of business. People lost their savings. Millions of people lost their jobs. Those who had jobs worked for a lot less. Many people suffered. They lost their homes. They became poor. They starved. Americans waited in long breadlines. They went to soup kitchens. They begged for food.

President Herbert Hoover was blamed for the Great Depression. He thought the economy would fix itself. He later provided government support. But it was too late. Things got bad. In 1932, Franklin D. Roosevelt was elected president. He hosted "fireside chats" to restore public confidence. He reformed banks. He reformed the stock market. Most importantly, he created jobs.

CAST of CHARACTERS

NARRATOR: person who helps tell the story

TOM MALLORY: a steel mill worker who lost his job and joined the **Civilian Conservation Corps** (CCC)

ARTHUR MAXWELL: an economist who works at the Department of **Commerce**

PRESIDENT HERBERT HOOVER: the 31st president of the United States

CLARA JENNINGS: a 12-year-old girl whose rich father lost his job

MRS. JENNINGS: mother of Clara Jennings

BACKSTORY
SPOTLIGHT BIOGRAPHY

Mary McLeod Bethune lived from 1875 to 1955. She was born in South Carolina. She was the daughter of former slaves. During the Great Depression, she served as the director of Negro Affairs of the National Youth Administration. She focused on education, training, and jobs. African Americans suffered more than white Americans. Bethune helped advocate for them. She made sure money was given to black education programs. She also made sure African Americans had access to jobs. In 1936, she became the highest-ranking African American woman in government. She did much for African Americans. She was an educator. She was a human rights leader. She founded a black college. She was a voice for African Americans.

Vocabulary
Civilian Conservation Corps
(suh-VIL-yuhn kahn-sur-VAY-shuhn KOR)
public work relief program that gave millions of young men jobs during the Great Depression

commerce (KAH-murs)
trade

FLASH FACT!
President Herbert Hoover led the country at the beginning of the Great Depression.

ACT 1

NARRATOR: TOM MALLORY *is talking to* **ARTHUR MAXWELL**. *They're at a government office.*

TOM: I'm here for a job.

ARTHUR: What type of job?

TOM: Any job. I'll do anything. I'm a hard worker. I'm a fast learner.

ARTHUR: What job skills do you have?

TOM: I worked at a steel mill. But my pa and I lost our jobs. Then, the mill closed. I don't know what we're going to do for food and **shelter**. We're running out of money.

ARTHUR: Things are getting really bad.

TOM: Many of our neighbors are having the same problems. Do you know what is happening?

Vocabulary
shelter (SHEL-tur) a place offering protection from the weather, like a home

FLASH FACT!
Many families couldn't pay their mortgages and rent. They got kicked out of their homes.

ARTHUR: I collect and study **employment** numbers. Earlier in 1929, everything was great. There were plenty of jobs. The stock market was strong. Prices were good.

TOM: Not everyone was doing well. Farmers struggled. Their crops were at low prices.

ARTHUR: I thought things were going to get better for farmers. The numbers were looking good.

TOM: Then what happened?

ARTHUR: The stock market crashed. This surprised everyone. The value of stocks went way down. People started selling their stocks. Some stocks became worthless. People lost a lot of money. Banks lost money. People stopped spending.

TOM: Factories closed. And people like me lost our jobs. I blame Hoover for this.

Vocabulary
employment (em-PLOY-munt)
jobs

FLASH FACT!
Many factories and businesses shut down.

NARRATOR: ARTHUR MAXWELL *is talking to* PRESIDENT HERBERT HOOVER. *They're in the president's office.*

ARTHUR: Things are getting really bad. The American people are losing faith in you. Should the government do something?

HERBERT: I've been looking at your reports. Things will even out. Americans have always stood on their own. They don't want a government **handout**. The government should stay out of business affairs.

ARTHUR: I agree, Mr. President. The country will come out of this slump. We will endure.

NARRATOR: *Arthur and Herbert were wrong. The economy got worse. Banks failed. People went broke.* CLARA JENNINGS *and her mother,* MRS. JENNINGS, *are talking. They're at their house.*

CLARA: What's wrong, Mother?

LOCATION SHOOTING
REAL-WORLD SETTING

President Herbert Hoover got blamed for the Great Depression. Many shantytowns popped up. Shantytowns were areas where poor people lived in shacks. They were called Hoovervilles. This was a way to criticize Hoover. One of the largest and longest-standing Hooverville was in St. Louis, Missouri. During the Great Depression, about 5,000 homeless people built a town on the banks of the Mississippi River. They made shacks from barrels and tar paper. They used wood pieces and trash to build things. The Mississippi River flooded the area 3 times. People had to rebuild again. The St. Louis Hooverville became popular. People gave tours. They even sold popcorn. The St. Louis Hooverville also had its own mayor. It was destroyed in 1936.

Vocabulary
handout (HAND-out) something given free to a person in need

FLASH FACT!
People panicked. They rushed to get their money out of the banks. This was called bank runs.

MRS. JENNINGS: Father lost his business. We lost all of our money.

CLARA: But I thought we were rich.

MRS. JENNINGS: We were. But not anymore. We will have to change our lives. We'll have to fire the **servants**. Your brother won't be able to go to college. He'll have to find work instead.

CLARA: What about our house?

MRS. JENNINGS: We'll have to sell our house. We need to **downsize**.

Vocabulary
servants (SUR-vuhnts)
people who work for other people

downsize (DOUN-size)
to get something smaller

FLASH FACT!
People waited in long lines for bread and other free items.

CLARA: It sounds like we'll have to learn to live with less.

NARRATOR: MRS. JENNINGS, CLARA JENNINGS, *and* TOM MALLORY *are at the breadline.*

CLARA: Mother, why are we in this line?

MRS. JENNINGS: We need food. This is a line to get free food.

CLARA: There are so many people in line. I see people who used to work for Father in this line.

MRS. JENNINGS: The Great Depression made us all poor. Hunger makes people equal. We're all the same.

TOM: It's tough times for everyone. I can't wait to vote Hoover out of office. He's the reason for all of this.

NARRATOR: ARTHUR MAXWELL *and* **HERBERT HOOVER** *continue their conversation in the president's office.*

ARTHUR: Maybe we should pay unemployed people?

HERBERT: We can't spend money we don't have. I don't want to run up a big **debt**. The government should stay out of it. Churches and neighbors should help people in need. Americans should take care of Americans.

ARTHUR: We have to do something. People are going hungry.

Vocabulary
debt (DET) money owed

FLASH FACT!
Some homeless people built shack communities.

ACT 2

NARRATOR: *At the end of his* **term**, **HERBERT HOOVER** *provided some government help. But he had stepped in too late. The country was in bad shape. People were homeless. The economy was getting worse.* **ARTHUR MAXWELL** *and Herbert are talking.*

ARTHUR: I'm sorry you lost the election to Franklin D. Roosevelt. I know you tried. The **dam** project on the Colorado River will be a big help. It'll bring water to the Southwest. And it will create new jobs.

HERBERT: I also gave out loans. These loans can help businesses and farmers.

ARTHUR: I hope President Roosevelt finishes some of the things you started.

HERBERT: I may no longer be president. But I'm still an American. I hope he's able to lead us out of the Great Depression.

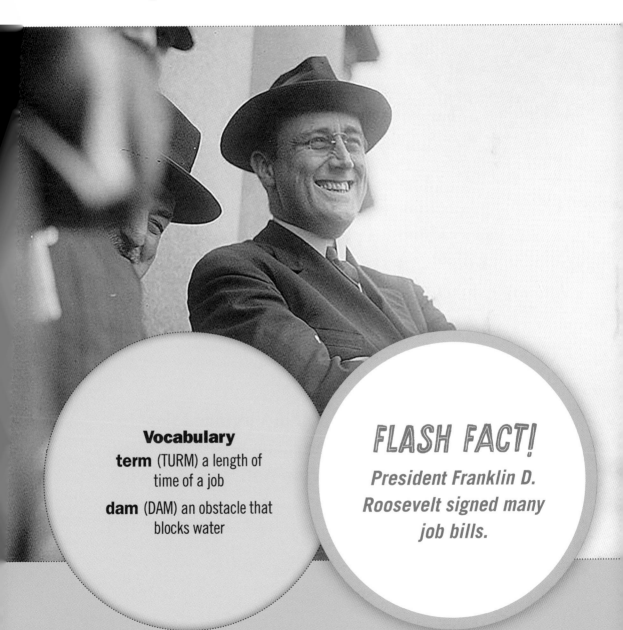

Vocabulary

term (TURM) a length of time of a job

dam (DAM) an obstacle that blocks water

FLASH FACT!

President Franklin D. Roosevelt signed many job bills.

NARRATOR: TOM MALLORY *and* **ARTHUR MAXWELL** *meet in a government building. Tom has just returned from basic training.*

TOM: Hey, Arthur, thanks for letting me know about President Roosevelt's new jobs program.

ARTHUR: I'm glad you signed up for the Civilian Conservation Corps. The U.S. Army is in charge of it.

TOM: The program is perfect for me. It gives men who are 18 to 25 years old jobs. It pays $30 a month. It also provides room and **board**. My family really needed this money. This will help us a lot.

ARTHUR: How was training?

TOM: I trained at Camp Roosevelt in Virginia. I slept in **barracks**. I wore uniforms. I woke up before dawn every day. I did exercises. I ate at a **mess hall**. I went to work. I built cabins.

Vocabulary

board (BORD) food provided as part of payment for work

barracks (BAR-uhks) a building in which soldiers lived

mess hall (MES HAL) cafeteria

FLASH FACT!

Government posters advertised jobs through work programs.

ARTHUR: Where are they going to send you? I heard they send men all over the country to work on public projects.

TOM: I'm going to be working at the Lincoln National Forest in New Mexico. I'll be traveling through Oklahoma and Texas. I've never been there before.

ARTHUR: That land has been **devastated** by the Dust Bowl. There used to be farms. But it's just dirt piles now. The Corps will be doing a lot of good work there.

TOM: I'm thankful for the work.

Vocabulary

devastated (DEV-uh-stayt-id)
destroyed and ruined

erosion (ih-ROH-zhuhn)
the gradual wearing away of soil or land by water or wind

FLASH FACT!

Young men worked at a CCC logging camp in Michigan in 1934.

ARTHUR: What are you going to be doing?

TOM: I will be working on **erosion**-control projects. I'll build small dams. This is to slow the water when it rains. I'll also be planting trees.

ARTHUR: Oh, you're part of Roosevelt's Tree Army!

TOM: Yes, I am! We're called soil soldiers! I can't wait. I'll be doing something important. And I'll be able to send money home. Things are looking up!

NARRATOR: CLARA JENNINGS *and* MRS. JENNINGS *are in their small room. Mrs. Jennings is sewing.*

MRS. JENNINGS: Did you finish your **chores**?

CLARA: I cleaned the kitchen. I made the beds. I cooked dinner. Tonight, we're having soup with a few vegetables. We don't have enough money for meat.

MRS. JENNINGS: You've been a great help. Your helping around the house lets me make money from sewing. We all have to do what we can.

CLARA: I never saw you sew before. I didn't know you could do that.

BLOOPERS
HISTORICAL MISTAKES

People thought President Herbert Hoover didn't do enough to help ease the Great Depression. He didn't want the government to step in. He wanted to encourage volunteerism. This means Americans should volunteer to help one another. But Americans wanted help. They didn't like Hoover. They thought he was out of touch with their troubles. They made jokes about him. "Hooverisms" became popular. These are words used to blame Hoover for the Great Depression. There are many examples. "Hoover blankets" are newspapers used to protect homeless people from the cold. "Hoover hogs" are rabbits hunted for food. "Hoover cars" are wagons pulled by mules. "Hoover flags" are empty pockets turned out. "Hoover bags" are small bags used to carry all of one's stuff. "Hoover shoes" are shoes with cardboard as soles.

Vocabulary
chores (CHORZ) small jobs

FLASH FACT!
CCC workers fought a forest fire in Wyoming in 1937.

MRS. JENNINGS: I used to work before I married your father.

CLARA: What happened to our car?

MRS. JENNINGS: Your father had to sell it. We're going to have to move again.

CLARA: Again? Why?

MRS. JENNINGS: It's too expensive to live in the city. And your father can't find a job here. My sewing doesn't bring in enough money.

CLARA: Where would we go?

MRS. JENNINGS: We'll move in with my parents. They have a lot of land outside of the city.

CLARA: But we don't know how to farm!

MRS. JENNINGS: We'll learn. We'll grow our own food. We'll raise chickens and pigs.

CLARA: We'll **survive** the Great Depression.

Vocabulary
survive (sur-VIVE)
to live through something hard

FLASH FACT!
The government encouraged families to can food.

EVENT TIMELINE

March 4, 1929: Herbert Hoover becomes president.

October 24, 1929: Wall Street crash starts.

October 29, 1929: Wall Street crashes. It's called Black Tuesday.

June 17, 1930: Smoot-Hawley Tariff Act passes. Tariffs are taxes on imported goods. It is supposed to help farmers. But other countries don't like it. It starts a trade war.

September–October 1930: First major round of U.S. banks fail.

December 11, 1930: Bank of United States fails. It is a private bank in New York. It's the country's fourth-largest bank. This is the largest bank failure in history at that time. It causes a bank panic.

1931: A severe drought hits the Great Plains. It's called the Dust Bowl. Crops die. "Black blizzards" begin. Dust from the overworked land begins to blow. The drought hits 23 states.

June 6, 1932: The Revenue Act of 1932 passes. It raises taxes. This makes the Great Depression worse.

November 8, 1932: Hoover loses to Franklin D. Roosevelt.

March 9, 1933: Roosevelt launches the New Deal with the Emergency Banking Act. The act restores confidence in banks.

March 31, 1933: The Civilian Conservation Corps is created. It's a public works relief program. It gives people jobs working on public lands.

April 19, 1933: Roosevelt ends the gold standard. This was a system that determined how much printed money was worth. It depended on a fixed amount of gold. He orders everyone to trade gold for dollars.

November 9, 1933: The Civil Works Administration is created. It gives jobs to 4 million people. On May 6, 1935, it became the Works Progress Administration (WPA). The WPA gives jobs to 8.5 million people.

August 15, 1935: The Social Security Act passes. This provides money to the elderly and people in need.

June 1938: The economy starts to grow again.

September 1939: World War II begins. The government creates military jobs. The Great Depression ends.

CONSIDER THIS!

TAKE A POSITION! Learn more about President Herbert Hoover. Was Hoover to blame for the Great Depression? Argue your point with reasons and evidence.

SAY WHAT? Learn more about the Great Depression. Explain what caused it. Explain the effects it had. Describe how people's lives changed.

THINK ABOUT IT! What would happen to you if your parents lost their jobs? How would your lives be affected?

Learn More

Baxter, Roberta. *The Great Depression.* Ann Arbor, MI: Cherry Lake Publishing, 2015.

Favreau, Marc. *Crash: The Great Depression and the Fall and Rise of America.* New York, NY: Little, Brown and Company, 2018.

Pascal, Janet B., and Dede Putra (illustr.). *What Was the Great Depression?* New York, NY: Grosset & Dunlap, 2015.

INDEX

ABOUT THE AUTHOR

Dr. Virginia Loh-Hagan is an author, university professor, and former classroom teacher. Popular foods during the Great Depression were hot dogs and potatoes. Virginia loves hot dogs and potatoes! She lives in San Diego with her very tall husband and very naughty dogs. To learn more about her, visit www.virginialoh.com.